UNDERWATER
PUPPIES

Also by Seth Casteel

Underwater Dogs

BEAR Shih Tzu/Poodle, 14 weeks

POPSICLE Puggle Mix, 9 weeks

UNDERWATER PUPPIES

Seth Casteel

LITTLE, BROWN AND COMPANY
New York Boston London

Little, Brown and Company
Hachette Book Group
237 Park Avenue, New York, NY 10017
littlebrown.com

First Edition: September 2014

Little, Brown and Company is a division of Hachette Book Group, Inc. The Little, Brown name and logo are trademarks of Hachette Book Group, Inc.

The publisher is not responsible for websites (or their content) that are not owned by the publisher.

The Hachette Speakers Bureau provides a wide range of authors for speaking events. To find out more, go to hachettespeakersbureau.com or call (866) 376-6591.

The on-land photos of the puppies are a collaborative effort from Seth Casteel and the puppies' parents.

ISBN 978-0-316-25489-2 (hc) / 978-0-316-29729-5 (Scholastic edition)
Library of Congress Control Number 2014937388

10 9 8 7 6 5 4 3 2 1

SC

Design by Gary Tooth/Empire Design Studio

Printed in China

I dedicate this book to puppies everywhere. Thank you for sharing your love and bringing smiles to our faces.

CONTENTS

x Introduction

1 Underwater Puppies

112 The Puppies on Land

115 Acknowledgments

116 About Seth Casteel

INTRODUCTION

Puppies inspire an overwhelmingly positive reaction in so many of us. We are drawn to puppies because of their appearance and are captivated by their personalities as we watch them explore the world. It's exhilarating because, unlike human babies, puppies become adults in just a few short months. Since they develop so quickly, it's especially important to savor our time with them and to ensure that, during this window, we as puppy parents are doing the right things to prepare them to be part of our world.

If you decide you would like a puppy in your life, then you have to be ready to prime that puppy for a variety of places and situations. The more we can expose our puppies to the world when they are young, the more we will see their experiences reflected in their confidence and happiness as adults.

Puppies Know How to Swim???

Puppies already know how to swim even at just a few weeks old. Some are more successful than others, but they all need practice to better understand their physicality, which improves their overall swimming ability. Swimming may be innate, but dogs didn't evolve with the luxury of swimming pools; since a swimming pool is not a natural body of water, there are different rules that apply. Natural bodies of water such as lakes, rivers, and oceans generally have a gradient, providing a simple way of exiting. Swimming pools usually have one exit, which is often a set of steps. If the puppy doesn't know where those stairs are, he is going to have trouble, so the most important thing to teach our puppies is how to get out of the pool on their own.

I think people make a mistake with their puppies and swimming when they assume their puppy can't swim and that the water is dangerous. In actuality, what these owners are doing is creating a hazardous scenario for the puppy by denying him his right to practice, especially in a swimming-pool situation.

When puppies reach a certain age, they become so curious that

they are fearless. During this time, it's important to develop these curiosities into confidence.

That's of course when it gets especially interesting for me. Seeing tiny puppies jump in on their own and swim to the ramp—it's incredible to watch them do it! In this book, among a range of underwater puppy experiences, you will see photographs of twelve-week-old Yellow Labrador Retrievers voluntarily diving to the bottom of a four-foot swimming pool to retrieve toys!

Rescue Puppies
It was important to me to feature dozens of adoptable and adopted puppies in this book to remind people that adoption is a fantastic option when considering bringing a puppy into your life. With a little research, you can find the type of rescue puppy you are looking for, pay a fraction of the price you would to a breeder, and save a life—a win-win-win! I want to thank all of the wonderful animal rescue organizations that made this book possible. Your tireless efforts to make the world a better place for animals is inspiring!

Do You Really Want a Puppy?
As much as we all love puppies, we aren't all necessarily in the ideal situation to care for one. So many people underestimate the responsibility involved. Before making your decision, you should also consider adopting a senior pet. These little friends have lived and learned and are generally going to be much easier to integrate into your home. And they won't chew up your brand-new shoes or destroy the carpet, either!

Puppies in This Book
I met a first-grade teacher in Chicago and spoke with her about *Underwater Puppies*. She told me that one of the reasons she is a first-grade teacher is that she has the privilege of witnessing important moments in her students' lives. She asked me, "How do you feel with the puppies?"

I said, "I feel like a first-grade teacher!" I experience so much pride when watching puppies swim for the first time. They've learned something they'll benefit from for the rest of their lives.

The puppies in the following photographs were ages six weeks to six months when I swam with them. Each puppy received swimming lessons to help prepare him to be part of the book and the world. I photographed more than a thousand puppies throughout the United States to achieve this collection of photographs.

UNDERWATER
PUPPIES

MARLOWE Vizsla, 10 weeks

PRINCE Boxer, 8 weeks

BLANCO American Pit Bull Terrier, 7 weeks

PANSY American Pit Bull Terrier, 7 weeks

DANTE Shar-Pei Mix, 9 weeks

RUGER Black Labrador Retriever, 7 weeks

BRANDO American Pit Bull Terrier, 8 weeks

GRITS Yellow Labrador Retriever, 12 weeks

HIPPIE Dalmatian, 6 months

TITAN Yellow Labrador Retriever, 5 months

DAPHNE Cavalier King Charles Spaniel, 16 weeks

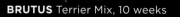

BRUTUS Terrier Mix, 10 weeks

SUGAR Boxer, 7 weeks

EMMY American Pit Bull Terrier, 14 weeks

CLYDE Black Labrador Retriever/Staffordshire Terrier, 16 weeks

ORBIT Cavalier King Charles Spaniel, 10 weeks

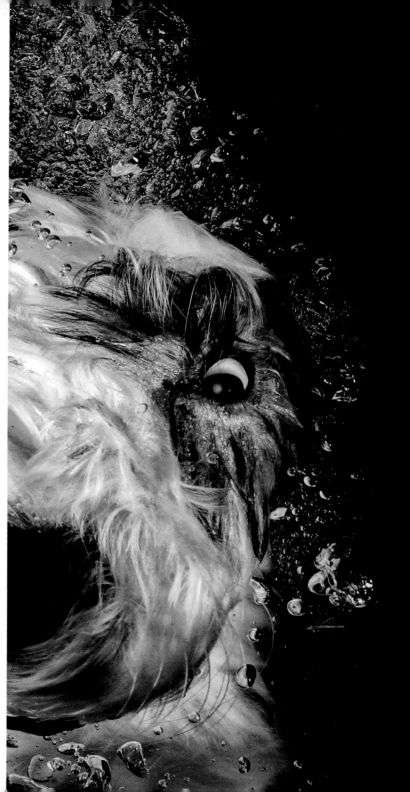

HAYMISH Old English Sheepdog, 10 weeks

LUMPKIN English Bulldog/Boston Terrier, 18 weeks

RAMONA German Shepherd Mix, 9 weeks

MALCOLM Miniature Pinscher, 9 weeks

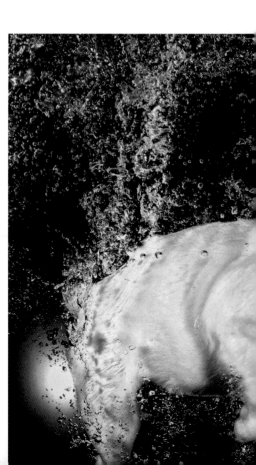

PIERRE American Pit Bull Terrier, 7 weeks

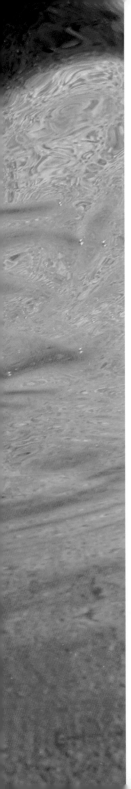

IGGY Pug, 15 weeks

PLUTO Italian Greyhound, 18 weeks

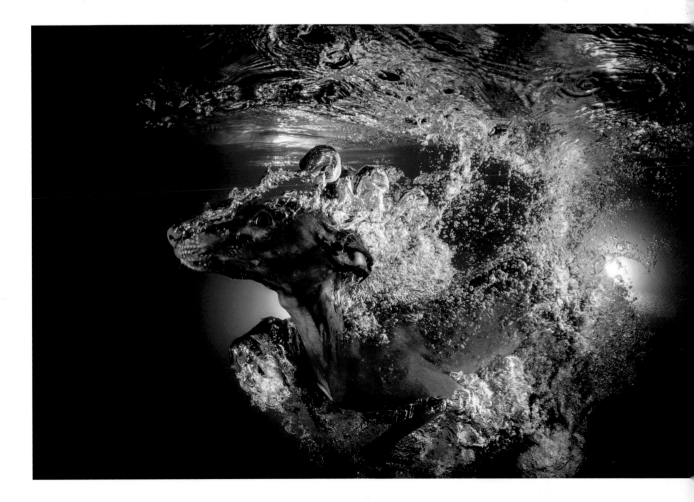

PRINGLES and **PICKME** Terrier Mixes, 8 weeks

PRINGLES Terrier Mix, 8 weeks

ROLLEY Terrier Mix, 10 weeks

CARU Chihuahua Mix, 6 weeks

BENTLEY French Bulldog, 16 weeks

GRIZZLE Chihuahua Mix, 6 weeks

BUTTERBALL Saint Bernard, 8 weeks

COREY Labrador Retriever/Australian Cattle Dog, 8 weeks

AVA Beagle Mix, 6 weeks

BARCELONA Goldendoodle, 11 weeks

GRACIE Border Collie Mix, 11 weeks

MALONE American Pit Bull Terrier Mix, 10 weeks

CHEYENNE Golden Retriever, 14 weeks

SADIE Basset Hound Mix, 8 weeks

DORA Dalmatian, 16 weeks

REASON Yellow Labrador Retriever, 12 weeks

DOUGLAS Shih Tzu, 8 weeks

ASPEN English Bull Terrier, 16 weeks

CHARLIE Chocolate Labrador Retriever, 17 weeks

JAX Yorkshire Terrier Mix, 17 weeks

JACK Yellow Labrador Retriever, 12 weeks

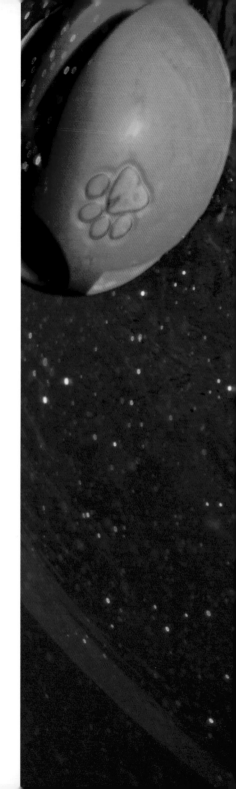

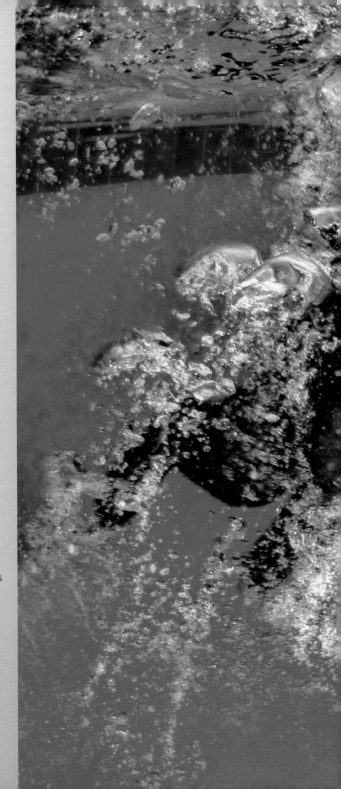

DUNCAN Chocolate Labrador Retriever, 9 weeks

NEVEL Russian Terrier, 8 weeks

IRIS American Pit Bull Terrier, 7 weeks

LUNA Beagle Mix, 10 weeks

PEPPER Vizsla, 16 weeks

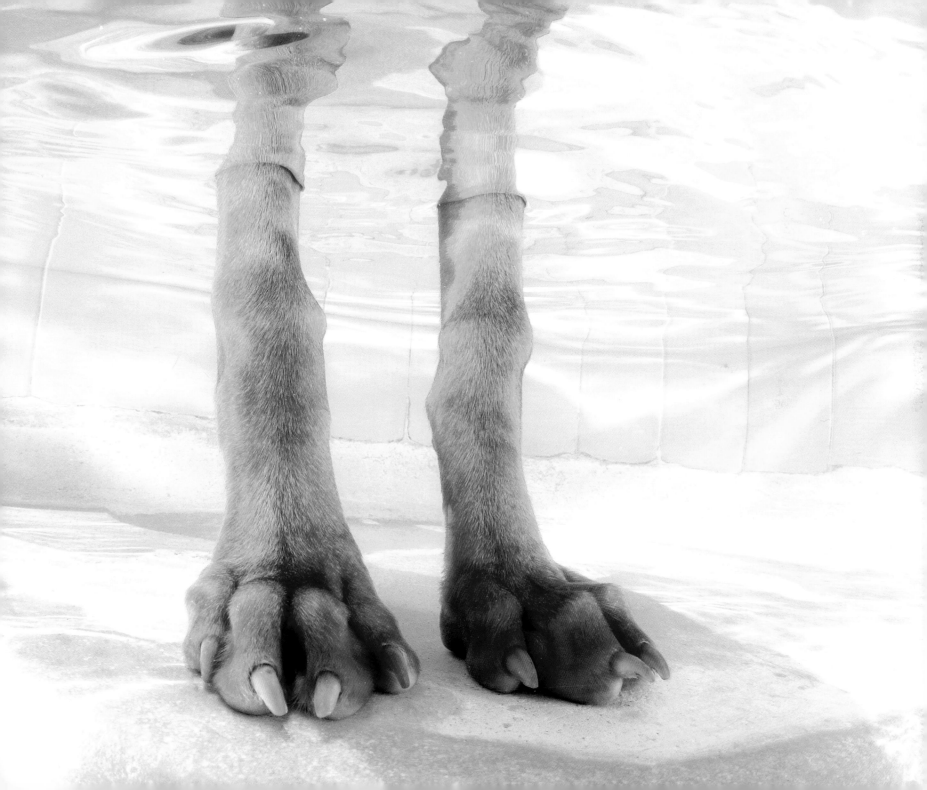

POPSICLE Puggle Mix, 9 weeks

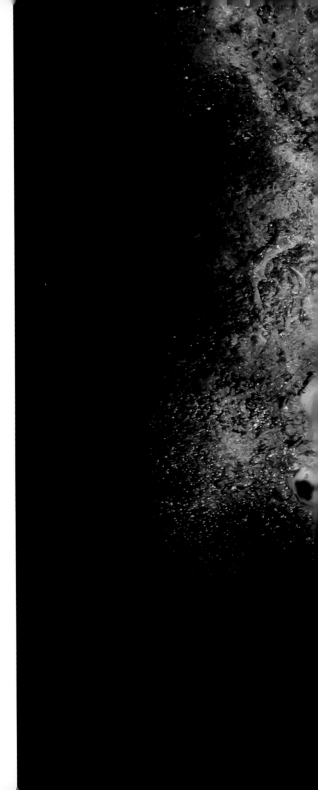

RACHEL German Shepherd Mix, 9 weeks

MILLER Boxer, 7 weeks

ALEX Terrier Mix, 10 weeks

ROO Toy Australian Shepherd, 13 weeks

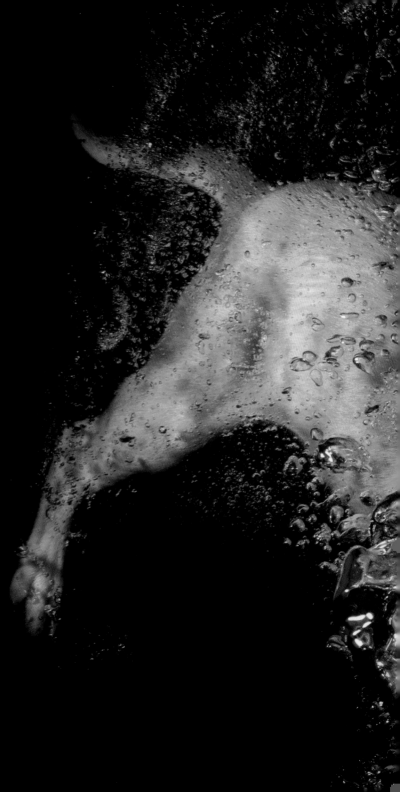

PANCAKE Puggle Mix, 9 weeks

BEAR Shih Tzu/Poodle, 14 weeks

RITZIE German Shepherd Mix, 9 weeks

GINGER Border Collie Mix, 12 weeks

AVI Australian Shepherd/Husky, 5 months

BLAZE American Pit Bull Terrier, 7 weeks

JETT Border Collie, 20 weeks

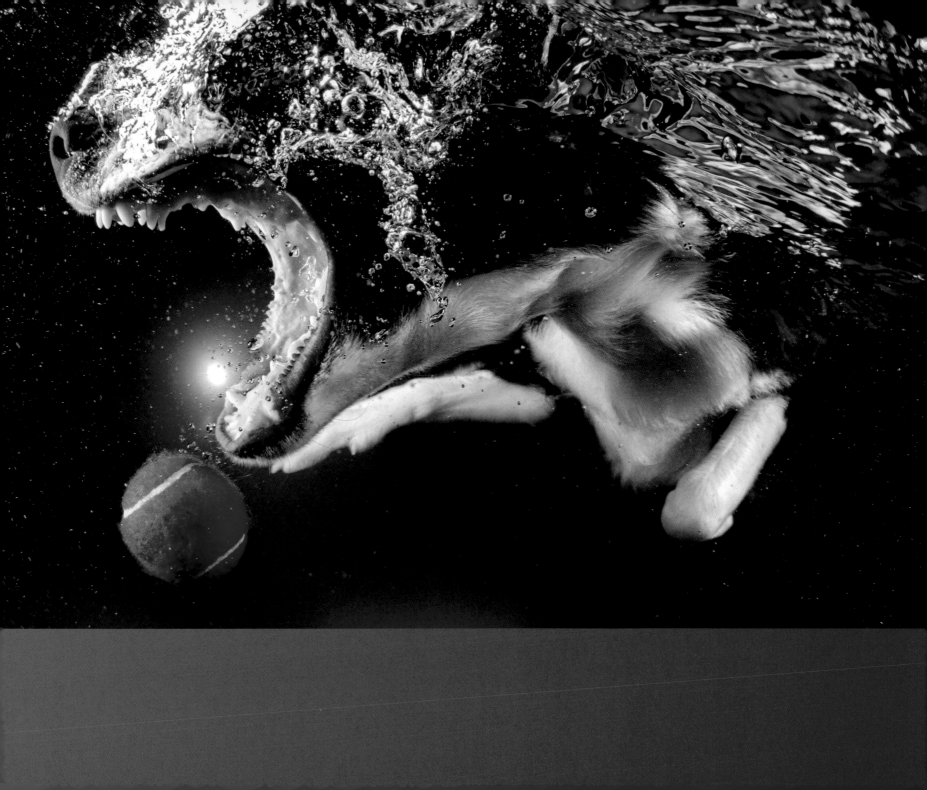

PAUL American Pit Bull Terrier, 16 weeks

GRITS and **REASON** Yellow Labrador Retrievers, 12 weeks

ZELDA Labrador Retriever/Australian Cattle Dog, 8 weeks

LUNA Border Collie/Labrador Retriever, 18 weeks

ALEX

ASPEN

ATTICUS

AVA

AVI

BARCELONA

BEAR

BELLA

BENTLEY

BLANCO

BLAZE

BRANDO

BRUTUS

BUTTERBALL

CARU

CHARLIE

CHEYENNE

CLYDE

COREY

DANTE

DAPHNE

DORA

DOUGLAS

DUNCAN